DATE DUE

Fine Pasta Food!

Rib Stickin Good!

Patty's Paste Palace

WELCOME!

written by
Phyllis Hofberg
& Lisa Galipeau

illustrated by
Phyllis Hofberg

ISBN: 0-7871-1162-7

Printed in Mexico.

A Dove Kids Book
A Division of Dove Entertainment
8955 Beverly Boulevard
Los Angeles, CA 90048

Distributed by Penguin USA

First printing: April 1997

10 9 8 7 6 5 4 3 2 1

To everyone I love , . . .
and to Patsy—thanks for showing up!

- Phyllis

Hey! There's Sidney and Herman!
And there's Mr. Rogers...
There's Fatman and Slobbin –
And the old Brooklyn codgers!
There's Chuey the Cheese Boy,
And real smelly Alice...

Appetizers to start with . . .
Have paste peas on paste toast!
Oh, do splurge on paste oysters—
—Just flown in from the Coast!

Then paste salad with dressing—
Would you care for paste soup?
It's our Cream Paste & Pill Bug,
Made with fresh pastey goop!

Would you care for a drink?...
Have a paste-powder milkshake,
Or paste juice from our sink!

Slurp on Paste-flavored Soda!
Guzzle Paste-booger Wine!...

Wipe your mouth!
Clear the table!
'Cuz it's Paste Dessert time!

Try some swarming paste flies
Mashed on sticky paste tarts!

Gobble muddy paste pies
Filled with frozen paste parts.

Have a scoop of paste custard,
Or a French Paste Brûlée.
Or paste ice cream with mustard
Or paste Dog-Doo Flambé!

This is just pretend food...
EATING PASTE MAKES YOU SICK!